A STEP-BY-STEP BOOK ABOUT
FINCHES

ELAINE RADFORD

Photography:
Dr. Herbert R. Axelrod; G. Ebben; Joshua Charap and Herschel Fray; Michael Gilroy; Ray Hanson; Paul Kwast; A. J. Mobbs; Mervin F. Roberts; William Starika; A. van den Nieuwenhuizen; Louise van der Meid; Norma Veitch; courtesy of Vogelpark Walsrode.
  Humorous drawings by Andrew Prendimano.

Distributed in the UNITED STATES by T.F.H. Publications, Inc., One T.F.H. Plaza, Neptune City, NJ 07753; in CANADA to the Pet Trade by H & L Pet Supplies Inc., 27 Kingston Crescent, Kitchener, Ontario N2B 2T6; Rolf C. Hagen Ltd., 3225 Sartelon Street, Montreal 382 Quebec; in CANADA to the Book Trade by Macmillan of Canada (A Division of Canada Publishing Corporation), 164 Commander Boulevard, Agincourt, Ontario M1S 3C7; in ENGLAND by T.F.H. Publications Limited, Cliveden House/Priors Way/Bray, Maidenhead, Berkshire SL6 2HP, England; in AUSTRALIA AND THE SOUTH PACIFIC by T.F.H. (Australia) Pty. Ltd., Box 149, Brookvale 2100 N.S.W., Australia; in NEW ZEALAND by Ross Haines & Son, Ltd., 18 Monmouth Street, Grey Lynn, Auckland 2, New Zealand; in SINGAPORE AND MALAYSIA by MPH Distributors (S) Pte., Ltd., 601 Sims Drive, #03/07/21, Singapore 1438; in the PHILIPPINES by Bio-Research, 5 Lippay Street, San Lorenzo Village, Makati Rizal; in SOUTH AFRICA by Multipet Pty. Ltd., 30 Turners Avenue, Durban 4001. Published by T.F.H. Publications, Inc. Manufactured in the United States of America by T.F.H. Publications, Inc.

CHOOSING

In most cases, you should buy your finches in pairs. All finches are social birds that require interaction with other finches in order to stay happy and healthy. With many species, you will be able to choose a male and a female. However, in some species, both sexes look alike, and you won't be certain that you've chosen one female and one male. Unless you want to try breeding, don't worry. Two males or two females kept together will usually become fast friends that can entertain each other just fine.

If you do want to try breeding for the first time, I suggest you start with a species that's dimorphic (males and females look different). Later, when you're more experienced, you can try working with the monomorphic species. In that situation, you will probably purchase at least six or eight birds and then set them up in a large aviary where they can find their own partners. It's true that there's a tiny chance that all six birds will be members of one sex, but the odds are overwhelmingly against such outstanding bad luck!

You can buy finches at a pet store or from a breeder. The size of the shop doesn't matter. What IS important is the seller's care and cleanliness. Are the perches, cups, and drinkers reasonably clean? Does the bottom of the cage look like it has been cleaned in the last 24 hours? Are the birds and cages scent-free? Remember that finches are naturally clean, neat birds. If they are kept under such poor conditions that they smell bad, they're not going to be healthy enough to withstand the stress of moving to a new home. Let the seller clean up his act before you buy.

Facing Page:
Amandava subflava, the Gold-Breasted Waxbill is the smallest of the waxbills, and enjoys the best quality high-protein foods.

6

If you think you will buy your finches from a small breeder, go ahead and get the cage from the pet store. You don't want your birds sitting around the house in a dark cardboard box waiting for their new home to arrive.

Once you've established that you're in good hands, you must still try to pick the strongest, most robust finches that you can. Never buy a feather-picked, torpid little bird out of pity! The stress of being captured and moved to a strange person's house isn't what a sick, weak finch needs.

The bird you were watching isn't necessarily the one that ended up in the seller's net, so always check over the finch *after* it has been caught. Does it have reasonably neat plumage and all of its toes? Are beak, eyes, and vent clear? Did it make a reasonable effort to evade capture? (Most healthy finches aren't crazy about being netted, you know, so it could be a sign of sickness if a bird in that situation doesn't seem alarmed.) If the bird looks OK except for a damp vent, it has probably just soiled itself under stress. However, since you don't know for sure that the finch isn't ill, I always request another bird anyway.

The Java Sparrow, *Lonchura oryzivora*, is sometimes called Java Rice Bird and is one of the hardiest of the larger finches.

Diamond Firetails, *Emblema guttata*, are coveted, but hard-to-find natives of Australia.

Since the finches may refuse to eat for several hours after moving to their new home, they must also be robust enough to withstand a possible weight loss. Fortunately, it's easy to determine whether or not a given bird is underweight. Gently feel the keelbone, the supportive bone that runs down the length of the breast. If it isn't padded by sufficient fat, the bone will feel knife-sharp under the feathers.

If you're buying a lot of finches or some of the relatively expensive species, you will probably want to have a vet examine your new birds within a few days after purchase. Many sellers will replace the birds if the vet finds a problem within a reasonable amount of time. However, you will be wise to get any guarantees in writing at the time of sale.

Just in case, keep your new finches in a room separate from any birds you may already own for two weeks to a month after bringing them home. That way, if your newcomers do turn out to have a disease, you won't have exposed your healthy pets.

By the way, don't let my mention of standard precautions scare you away from finches. Despite the possibility of disease that occurs when you buy any living thing, I must object to the popular idea that finches are touchy little things that die at the drop of a hat. With what we know today about diet and care, you should plan on enjoying your finches for many years.

Small birds don't necessarily mean small cages. Finches exercise by flying, not by climbing the way that parrots do, so they usually need a bit more room than you'd expect. Pet stores, reasoning that they're holding the birds for only a short time, often display finches in small one foot by one foot

HOUSING

cages. That doesn't mean you can keep your finches in such a cage permanently—any more than you'd expect a dog to live out its life in something the size of a puppy display cage.

Granted, you can get away with keeping a pair of finches in a cage that small—if you're willing to let the birds fly around a birdproof room for at least an hour a day. I promise you, after you've had to catch the finches a few times to return them to their cage, you won't be willing. However, if you must go this route, I suggest that you schedule free-flight time at night. That way, you can turn off the lights and completely darken the room when you are ready to pick up the finches and return them to their cage. (They won't fly in the low light of a nightlight.) In general, though, I suggest you leave super-small cages for single budgies that spend a great deal of time outside their cages playing with their owners. Give your finches at least three cubic feet of space per pair.

Since finches don't chew their cages, you have a lot of choices when it comes to design. I have kept finches happy and healthy in cages made of bamboo, wood, hardware cloth, and even the remains of an old computer cabinet. However, I am sorry to report that most antique and so-called decorator cages are either too small or too flimsy for a pair of active finches. My imported bamboo cage was reduced to toothpicks after about a year of moderately hard use. If you want to buy a cage, go to the experts; a pet store or pet supply house will have a better idea of what your finch needs than does the guy you run into at a garage sale.

If you are handy or can get the cooperation of someone who is, you can build yourself a perfectly adequate cage

Neochmia ruficauda, the Star Finch, is a very cheerful singer with a pretty warble and varied song.

with clips and welded wire. If you want a very large cage, you will get a very sturdy design by building a metal, wood, or PVC frame. Of course, you should make sure that any paint or other chemicals used on your building materials are lead and toxin-free. Avoid "treated" woods, and paint over questionable surfaces with several layers of leadfree paint. Note: You will find it much easier to see into the cage and enjoy your finches if you paint the welded wire with a safe brand of flat black.

A note about cage locations is in order. Finches require comfortable temperatures, clean air, a certain amount of peace and quiet, and freedom from drafts. For all these reasons, you should never place a finch cage in the kitchen. If the alternating blasts from the fridge door and heat from the oven doesn't get them, the smoke and cooking odors will. If you think a pretty brass cage is just the thing to hang in your kitchen, fill it with flowers! In general, the best place for a finch cage is a clean, draft-free area where the whole family can enjoy watching the birds without being forced to walk so close to the cage that they keep the finches in a constant state of alarm.

11

When choosing a cage for finches, be sure the space between the bars is small enough that your little jewels cannot escape.

Suppose you have more than two finches? In general, I suggest that you keep each pair in a separate cage to avoid pecking order conflicts. However, if you have a large flight cage—closet-sized or larger—you may certainly expect to keep several pairs together without fighting. In fact, given enough room, you will find that you can even add a budgie or a cockatiel to your showcase aviary. For instance, I have heard several people comment that budgies will break a Zebra finch's leg if both birds are kept in the same cage. Yet, in my closet-sized living room aviary, my Zebra finches rule the roost—and the budgie is so gentle he is often permitted to groom the male Zebra's head!

Can you keep finches in an outdoor aviary? Of course you can, if you live in a mild climate such as that found in southern California or Florida. However, there are some details that you should consider *before* you pour the concrete.

Zoning is first and foremost if you live in an urban or suburban neighborhood. Find out if you need a permit. Talk to your nearest neighbors about your aviary plans and gauge their reactions. Incredible as it seems to you and me, some people don't like birds. You might as well find out before you invest a lot of money in a structure you won't be allowed to use.

The second consideration is predators. Some of the smartest and most problematic predators—especially rats and cats—live in the city, so don't think you're immune. Nonpoisonous snakes, normally friends because they eat mice and rats, can also be a problem if they get into an aviary since finch makes a welcome change in their diets. To prevent problems, many people pour eighteen inch concrete floors under the outdoor aviaries. Others, who prefer to keep the natural earth floor, sink the aviary sides at least eighteen inches into the dirt.

Sadly, some predators are the two-footed kind. Any outdoor aviary system must have locks and alarms to deter vandals and thieves.

Finally, any outdoor aviary must have a covered shelter. Finches need a safe place to roost when storms or cold snaps threaten.

An aviary provides a most ideal environment for birds. A properly designed and constructed aviary will afford many happy hours of avicultural pleasure.

Finches in large flight cages and outdoor aviaries will get plenty of exercise. However, finches in smaller cages should be encouraged to "work out" with a limited selection of toys. A small swing is number one with most finches. Few things are more touching than the sight of two devoted finches trying to figure out how to sit side by side on a small swing—and few are more amusing than watching a gentle squabble over whose turn it is to go it alone. Other toys can be fun, too. You can be sure that any toy that's safe for a budgie is safe for a finch. Of course, you should never stuff the cage with so many toys that the finches don't have room to fly around.

The brilliantly colored canary, a result of careful selective breeding, is widely renowned for its beautiful singing.

HOUSING

Parson Finch. This small Australian bird measures only 4 ½ inches in length!

Other cage accessories include perches, nestboxes, and "bird protectors." The latter is a protective disk that should be hung outside the finch cage in order to prevent mites from taking up residence in your birds' feathers. These disks can be bought in pet stores and should be replaced at the recommended intervals.

The kind of perches you use is important to the health of your birds' feet—which in turn is crucial to the health of your bird. Remember, if a finch's feet hurt, it can't lie down for a nap! Most cages come supplied with perches, but you'll probably need to buy extras anyway. Replace any plastic perches at once; this material simply won't keep the birds' nails in trim the way wooden perches will.

For finches, you should choose the smallest diameter perches available. In general, the perch should be wide enough that the bird's toes don't wrap around on top of each other but not so wide that the bird can't get its toes three-quarters or one-half of the way around it. If you have a choice between several slightly different perches, get one of each kind so that your finches won't always have to sit the same way.

Natural branches from nonpoisonous trees make terrific perches—if you're sure that the tree in question hasn't been sprayed with insecticides for several years. Unfortunately,

15

that lets out the branches of most cultivated fruit trees. But if you can supply your finches with a green branch from an un-sprayed apple, birch, or willow tree, you will be giving them the benefits of toy, perch, and vitamin supplement all rolled up into one.

Since caged finches rarely exercise as much as aviary or wild birds, they may sometimes develop overgrown toenails despite your wisest perch choices. If so, you need to get the bird's nails trimmed as soon as possible. Otherwise, the bird may "catch" itself on a toy or a cage-bar join and injure itself trying to get free. Fortunately nail-clipping is quite easy. Your local pet store or groomer's will do the job for a small fee. You can also do it yourself.

Before you start, lay out all of your equipment: a pair of nail trimmers marketed for puppies or birds, a clean towel, a mister, a damp handrag, and a styptic powder such as Kwik-Stop. You may catch the finch in one of two easy ways, de-pending on the time of day. If it is late in the evening, you can simply turn off the lights and let the finch settle down in the darkness before reaching in carefully to pick it up with the clean towel. If it's relatively early, you can spray the finch with the mister until it's too damp to fly. I personally prefer the sec-ond method, because if I accidentally let the finch go, it's much easier to recapture. However, you should never soak a finch that's in less than excellent health. For that matter, if you sus-pect the finch isn't feeling well, you should probably not be subjecting it to the additional stress of grooming at this time.

You can hold a finch in one hand while clipping its nails with the other, but for the first few times you should prob-

Estrilda troglodytes, the Red-Eared Waxbill, is vivacious, gregarious, and peaceful.

Red-Eared Waxbills are very active African birds, and should be included in every collection of small finches.

ably have a partner hold the bird. Always wrap your hand around the bird's back and wings to prevent it from flapping and hurting itself in its excitement. Place your thumb on one cheek and your forefinger on the other to keep its head still. Never press on the bird's diaphragm, since such pressure could interfere with easy breathing.

Trim the nails as quickly as you can while still working safely. It's better to take off too little than too much, since repeating the job in another week or two is less stressful for the finch than accidentally cutting into a vein. If your finch has light-colored toes, you'll be able to easily avoid the dark vein because you can see where it ends in the translucent nail. If it has darker toes, you'll have to file or snip off the end of the nail with extreme care. However, don't panic if you do hit a vein. Simply get a little styptic powder on the damp towel and hold it against the bird's toe until the bleeding stops. The combination of these very effective powders and direct pressure usually stops bleeding in a matter of seconds.

Toys and perches will take care of your finches by day, while nestboxes or wicker baskets will keep them warm and cozy at night. Don't neglect to provide a nest just because you aren't interested in breeding your pets. Finches feel infinitely more secure if they can hide or sleep in an enclosed place.

Are cage covers necessary? I usually respond with a definitive maybe. Although probably not required in a quiet room where the birds aren't disturbed much in the evenings, covers can be a good way to tell finches in a busier area that it's time to settle down for the night. They also discourage late-

17

Zebra Finches are the darlings of the hobby.

night visitors from poking and prodding at birds who are trying to sleep. But if you do cover your birds, try to establish a routine so that the finches will be able to go to sleep at about the same time each night.

Keeping a finch cage clean is easy. Most people simply line the cage bottom with paper that's changed daily. Newspaper is a popular choice now that lead has been removed from the black ink; however, it's possible for light-colored birds to soil themselves on newsprint. I prefer to use undyed or white paper towels in cages where there's no grate separating birds from paper.

"Major" cleaning consists of wiping down soiled perches and cage bars once a week. It's best to use plain water, although you can add a teaspoon of chlorine bleach to a quart of water if you need the extra sterilizing power. If you still can't get the perches clean, use sandpaper or the special perch brushes sold in pet stores. Food and water dishes must, of course, be washed out each day before you refill them.

The finches themselves also enjoy regular cleansing. You can provide them with a bath that they can splash in at their leisure, or you can mist them with a gentle spray from a plant mister. You'll soon learn which method your finches like best.

18

Added to the pleasing appearance of the Zebra Finch is a friendly and delightful personality.

FEEDING

Feeding your finches is easy. These hardbilled birds thrive on a seed-based diet that's cheap, easy to store, and convenient to feed. Many of the most popular finches for beginners originated in dry, rather harsh climates in Africa and Australia, so they're well-adapted to simpler diets than a tropical rainforest dweller would demand. Furthermore, since Australia doesn't export its wildlife, any finch you buy with an Australian heritage is probably the product of many generations of birds used to eating a captive diet.

Yet, no finch can thrive on seed and water alone—not even the hardy Zebra finch, who would make a brave effort. Like any other animal, birds require protein, fat, carbohydrate, vitamins, and minerals in order to stay happy and healthy.

If any nutrient can be called more important than any other, it's protein. All animals require protein in order to grow and to repair damaged cells. Because it's so vital for growth, young birds and breeding birds have a special need for protein. However, any bird, even a spoiled pet, needs a certain amount of protein in order to resist disease and to replace its feathers when it molts.

Carbohydrates and fats are energy foods, the fuel the body runs on. Fat is a very concentrated form of energy that can be stored compactly in a bird's body for future use. It's also needed to keep the feathers smooth and shiny. However, since they don't have to spend a lot of energy hunting for food, captive birds easily consume too much fat. Obese birds run a greater risk of disease, so you'll want to avoid offering too many oily seeds and other fattening treats.

Carbohydrate is an easily-digested form of energy food that the bird's body can use quickly, without much need for prolonged digestion. Since you should store captive birds' ex-

Facing Page:
The beautiful Diamond Firetail is another of nature's
treasures originating in Australia.

Cuttlebone provides necessary calcium and should be available to the birds at all times.

cess calories in the cupboard rather than around their waists, you'll generally want to offer high-carbohydrate, low-fat seeds.

In addition to protein, fat, and carbohydrate, birds also need vitamins and minerals so that their bodies can use their food efficiently. A bird's body can make its own vitamin C and some of the B vitamins, but it must be fed sufficient quantities of vitamins A, D, and E in order to stay fertile and healthy. Of the minerals, calcium is most crucial because it's used in the formation of bones and eggs, in addition to serving several other functions in the body.

Of course, most nutritious foods contain varying combinations of several of these elements. So how do you make sure your finches are getting what they need to thrive without making them fat or driving yourself bananas?

The traditional diet makes a good start. In most situations, you can keep a good "finch mix" of seeds in front of the birds 24 hours a day. Since dry seed doesn't spoil very easily, you need to change the seed cup only once a day. Finch mix is designed to present a fairly balanced ratio of carbohydrate-rich and fat-rich seeds, and your finches will get plenty of energy from such a diet. During periods of special stress—the molt, breeding, or show conditioning—you can also offer seed combinations tailored for the extra calorie and nutritional requirements these situations demand.

22

FEEDING

Seed does lose nutritional value as it ages, and old, moldy seed does more harm than good. An insect or two is a harmless source of protein, but seed that's covered with dust, mold, or bugs should be tossed out. To make sure your seed is still alive, sprout a teaspoon or two occasionally. (Seed sprouters are available at health food stores. Follow the directions on the package.) If the seed doesn't sprout, it's too old. If the seed does sprout, feed these healthy young greens to your finches.

Most finches have a great fondness for millet. Millet spray delights them even more.

Two ways of giving seeds in treat form deserve special mention because they give finches exercise and pleasure in addition to nutrition. One treat consists of bunches of spray millet, with the heads of seeds still on the dried stalk. Just hang the spray at the top of the cage and watch the finches go! They can spend hours exploring the stalk for the delicious seeds. The other kind of treat, "toys" or sticks made of seeds and honey, can be a bit more fattening, so I tend to save it for special occasions unless I feel the finches may need the extra calories.

The remainder of the traditional diet includes greens, a bit of apple every few days, grit, and a mineral block or cuttlebone. I urge you to keep a clean mineral block or cuttlebone hanging in your finches' cage at all times, replacing it when it's used up or soiled. Don't write it off because the birds seem to go for weeks at a time without touching it. You can't predict ahead of time when the finches will feel a need for the extra calcium and attack the block with an appetite that will amaze you.

Grit is another important element of the diet, although it often puzzles beginners. Why feed a bird something that's no more and no less than crushed rocks? Actually, there are excellent reasons for keeping a teaspoon of clean grit in a treat cup in the finch cage. Because they don't have teeth to chew their food with, finches occasionally swallow a bit of grit to help grind up the food in their stomachs. In addition to making seeds easier to digest, grit can also provide a few essential minerals.

Pytilia melba, the stunning Melba Finch.

However, it has happened that a sick or stressed finch has "gone crazy" and continued eating grit until it died. For that reason, you should remove the grit cup if you think the finches are feeling stressed or ill. Since moving the cage or capturing a finch for a nail trimming is somewhat stressful, remove the grit cup for a day or two after you do these things.

The greens and apple, usually offered every other day or twice a week, represent token attempts at making sure the finches get enough vitamins and fiber. These foods are fine, but they're really not enough. Let's pause a second and take stock of the standard diet.

The seeds are full of energy and some assorted B vitamins, the mineral block offers vital minerals, and the grit eases digestion. But we're still missing sufficient quantities of protein and the A, D, and E vitamins. Without protein, the bird can't replace its feathers during the molt. Without the vitamins, it

A gorgeous pair of Red-Cheeked Cordon Bleu. If fed on mealworms and live foods, pairs usually can be counted on to breed fairly well.

can't keep its skeleton, breathing system, or fertility intact. In fact, without vitamins A and D, it can't even efficiently use the calcium you've given. Obviously, you're going to have to add something to the standard diet if you want to keep your finches around for years to come.

There are zillions of ways to add protein to the diet. In fact, a whole mystique has sprung up around protein. Beginners could conceivably toss up their hands and forget the whole thing after hearing a few experts pontificate on eggfood formulas, insect-catching, and other esoteric techniques. Actually, giving protein can be as simple or as complex as you care to make it.

The easiest way to offer protein is to obtain some game bird or turkey starter from a feed store. These scientifically formulated foods contain vitamins A and D in addition to protein and carbohydrate. (Don't offer chicken starter, since it contains medications that are bad for finches and most other birds.) If you live in an urban area and can't get to a feed store, you can offer dried dog food or mynah bird pellets instead. These foods must be grated briefly in a blender to reduce them to the crumble size that finches prefer. Use the pulse speed so that the device doesn't get carried away and reduce them to powder.

Since eggs are the most balanced and complete form of protein known, many experts like to give egg on a regular basis. Fortunately, you don't need a chemistry degree or a wizard to make a nutritious, attractive eggfood. Simply mash a hardboiled egg, mixing together the white and the yolk, and place it in the cage in its own treat cup. Since egg can spoil fairly quickly, remove the cup after an hour.

If you want to leave the egg out for a full 24 hours, you need to mix it with something that will make it a little drier and more resistant to spoilage. Breeders have discovered that a teaspoon each of brewer's yeast and powdered avian vitamins does the job nicely—and makes the egg even more nutritious! However, in hot weather, I would prefer to leave even this mix out for only 12 hours.

Beginners are unlikely to acquire finches that need live insects. However, if you do, you needn't think that you will be spending the rest of your life in your backyard chasing down crickets. The bird magazines regularly run advertisements from reputable businesses that will deliver healthy insects right to your door. Mealworms are especially popular because they will "hibernate" in the refrigerator for several weeks, allowing you to keep a supply of live insects on hand at all times.

The Owl Finch from Australia is also called the Bicheno Finch.

The Fawn-Breasted Waxbill, a native of Africa, is pleasant, hardy, and peaceful.

If your finches were bred by someone who offered the traditional low-protein diet, your birds may be suspicious of the new foods at first. In order to coax them into trying the high protein foods, you may have to remove the seed cup for a few hours. It might even be necessary to try this tactic several times over the course of a week or two before the finches become convinced that the eggfood or game bird starter is OK to eat. Be patient. You won't make your finches healthier by starving or giving up on them.

Robert G. Black, a leading expert on the nutrition of finches, feels that many or most pet birds don't get enough vitamins A and D. Since the problems caused by a deficiency of these vitamins can develop slowly over time, you may not be aware your birds are in trouble until it's too late. I strongly recommend that you supplement all seed-eating birds' diets with these important vitamins.

An old breeder's trick that works well is to add a teaspoon of vitamins A and D to a pound of seed and stir well. Let the vitamins soak into the seed for 24 hours before you begin

27

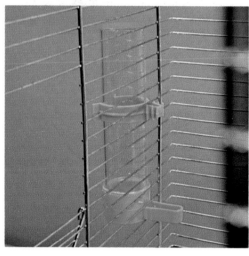

A water font helps to ensure a steady supply of fresh water so necessary for the health of your birds.

using it. Since these fat-soluble vitamins can spoil easily, keep the seed that you have treated this way in the refrigerator until you're ready to serve it to the birds.

Make sure that the vitamins you use come from animal sources. Vitamin supplements especially prepared for birds will be fine, but you must read the labels carefully if you pick up your A and D in a health food store. Human bodies can use a form of vitamin D that comes from vegetable sources, but birds' bodies can't. In my opinion, the vitamins derived from fish sources are best for both humans and finches.

Because fish oils do spoil quickly, never leave out treated seed for more than 24 hours! Have some untreated seed around to offer on those occasions when you think you might be gone overnight or for the weekend.

Birds kept outside get plenty of vitamin D, since this "sunshine vitamin" is also formed on the skin in reaction to sunlight. To give indoor finches this advantage, you can install full spectrum (NOT broad spectrum) fluorescent lights in the bird room or larger finch cage. Full spectrum bulbs are marketed under a variety of names, but they will stress the fact that they are healthy for humans and other animals because they mimic the wavelengths found in sunlight—including some

wavelengths that aren't visible to our eyes. Sometimes, if you're buying your fluorescent tubes in a store that mostly supplies offices, the sales literature will stress the fact that these bulbs make it easier to read or evaluate colors. Broad spectrum bulbs, on the other hand, have wavelengths that help plants grow but don't contain all the wavelengths needed by animals.

As you probably know, clean water should be kept in front of finches at all times. To prevent disease, wash out the drinker and change the water each day. Unless you're quite confident of the quality of your tap water, I wouldn't give it to your finches. In addition to the alphabet soup of strange chemicals that are finding their way into municipal water supplies and artesian wells, the chlorine used to kill infectious bacteria isn't especially good for small birds. Boiling the water will remove the chlorine, but not the chemicals, so at this point in time I'm giving my birds (and myself) distilled water. You might be wise to do the same.

The stunning Red-Billed Firefinch is probably the best breeder of the waxbills.

BREEDING

Breeding finches is fun, interesting activity that can be enjoyed by bird owners of all ages. It's difficult enough to present a healthy challenge, yet not so difficult that dedicated beginners can't get some results for their efforts. Children and adults alike receive considerable pleasure from helping their birds create new life. Furthermore, since there's no finch overpopulation problem, you can breed all the birds your heart desires without worrying about what you're going to do with them all. Even the prolific Zebra finch can be easily traded at many pet stores for seed and supplies.

Although it's important for more people to begin breeding the rarer species, beginners should start with reliable breeders such as Zebra or Society finches. Once you gain experience, you can move up to the more difficult birds. Since there are enough fascinating colors and patterns among these two species to keep a breeder busy for a lifetime, you won't be missing out by starting with the "common" birds.

Besides, if you become deeply involved in raising rare finches, you will find that a birdroom of Zebras or Societies is invaluable in saving many of your young exotics. As we'll see later, these species make hard-working parents that are willing to rear the young of touchier birds to healthy maturity.

If you wish to start small—perhaps with just one pair—I suggest you begin with Zebras. You can't tell what sex Societies are by looking at them, so it's easy to end up with male-male or female-female "pair" that goes through the motions of courtship without producing anything. Zebras, on the other hand, are easily sexed. In most varieties, the male can be distinguished from the female by the large orange patches on his cheeks. In the few varieties where the patch is absent in both sexes, the male usually possesses a bright red bill that

noticeably more colorful than the female's.

You should be aware that a single pair of Zebras (and many other finches) will take longer to settle down to breeding than three or four or more pairs kept in the same room or aviary. These social birds feel safer about investing the effort required to raise young when they know that other birds are doing the same thing. To encourage a lone pair to go to nest, you might want to tape them when they're making cheerful sounds for playback each day.

Don't breed your finches too young. Some species such as Zebras are such free breeders that a hen may start laying before she's three months old. Unfortunately, a bird that young is rarely strong or steady enough for successful breeding. In fact, if she hasn't had time to stockpile enough calcium and other nutrients in her body, she may even develop a dangerous condition called egg-binding. This condition, the inability to

One- and two-day-old finch chicks.

pass the egg, can be fatal, especially if the egg breaks inside her. And even if the very young hen does lay successfully, she's unlikely to feel like settling down to incubating eggs or feeding chicks. For best breeding results, don't encourage your finches to start until they are around eight months old.

While you're waiting for your finches to mature, you can decide whether cage breeding or aviary breeding is right for you. Both methods have their advantages and disadvantages. Which one you choose will depend on your space, energy, resources, and interests.

Many kinds of finches can be bred successfully in cages that are three or four cubic feet in volume. One pair per

The Strawberry Finch in courtship.

cage, please. If you try to place two or three pairs in a cage this size, you'll get squabbling, not breeding.

Cage breeding is often preferred by exhibitors and other serious breeders because you control who mates with whom. In the aviary, your best bird might mate with your worst, producing mediocre young. Using individual cages, you can guarantee that your two best birds will get together. You can also experiment with developing new types and colors that might never make an appearance in a busy aviary. You can also avoid pairing birds who could produce defective young; for instance, it's usually wise to prevent pure-white finches from mating with each other because some of their offspring could be blind.

Another important advantage of cage-breeding is that you'll find it easier to monitor the health of individual birds when they're kept in cages. In a large aviary, it's easy to overlook one sluggish bird hanging back in a dark corner. You'd notice the same bird's distress a lot sooner if it were one of only two finches in a cage. Furthermore, it's fairly easy to help a sick bird in a cage. If necessary, you can cover the cage in a dark towel and carry the whole thing to the vet's—infinitely easier on both you and the bird than trying to net it in its aviary. It's also easier to isolate sick birds from healthy ones when each pair is already in its own cage.

Erythrura trichroa, the Blue-Faced Parrot Finch.

Of course, breeding in cages also has its disadvantages. For one thing, it's usually more expensive to buy many small cages than it is to construct one large flight cage or aviary. It also takes much longer to clean and maintain multiple small cages. If you're extremely busy—and who isn't these days?—you'll find colony breeding much easier than cage breeding.

However you choose to breed, you must supply your finches with nests that make them feel secure before you can expect successful breeding. Although nests can be made from objects as arcane as milk cartons or as natural as coconut halves, there are basically two kinds of nests. The open-cup nest, often made of wicker, is well-liked by Zebras, Societies, Canaries, and other rather confident finches. Closed nests with openings on the side, often boxes made of wood, are favored by finches that might prefer nesting in tree-holes and the like in the wild.

34

BREEDING

If you aren't sure which kind of nest your finches will like best, give them one of each and let them choose. In the aviary situation, you should have one-and-a-half to two nests per pair in order to prevent unnecessary fighting. Most finches will be happiest with nests hung high in the cage.

Many finches like to line their own nests before they start to lay. Once they're old enough, you can give them a nudge in the right direction by providing plenty of safe nesting

Spice Finches are hardy, inexpensive, and peaceful. They are excellent for beginners.

material that won't get tangled up in their toes. Sterile goat hair, horsehair or down are all good materials. Dry, unsprayed grass or fresh hay are also popular. If you don't provide enough nest materials, the birds may pick themselves or each other for extra feathers, so don't be too stingy. A surprising amount of grass and duck down can go into one little Zebra nest!

You can also manage the lighting to let the finches know it's time to get busy. In general, if you gradually work up to 14 hours of light each day, the finches will think it's spring and turn their thoughts to courtship. Use a timer to turn the lights on and off on a regular schedule.

Diet must be watched most carefully before, during, and after breeding. Both parents must be in top-notch condi-

tion if they are to breed without exhausting themselves. Protein, vitamins A and D, and calcium must all be supplied in plentiful quantities to prevent such ills as egg-binding, chicks dying in the shell, weak chicks susceptible to disease, and other headaches which can ruin a breeding effort.

Many finches won't breed unless they're presented with a plentiful supply of protein. Perhaps they feel that breeding youngsters is just too much of a gamble to be worth the effort if certain high-quality foods aren't available. In any case, you may have to experiment a bit before you discover the trigger that will start your finches off. Many will be content with daily helpings of eggfood and game-bird starter. Others may hold out for live insects. Later, when we look at some individual species, I'll give you an idea of who is likely to turn fussy.

Once the hen begins laying, she will produce up to ten eggs at a rate of an egg every day or so. Beginners should restrain the urge to "help" by checking the eggs every ten minutes. Repeated interference may cause the birds to abandon the breeding project in disgust. Once you're experienced enough to be able to offer real assistance to an egg or chick in trouble, you can check the nest once or twice a day. When you're just starting out, though, the birds will probably know more than you do about how to bring up baby.

If you notice that one of your hens looks like she's straining to pass an egg, she's eggbound! You must act quickly, because her life is at stake. If she's already in a small cage, you can clip a lamp near one end for warmth. If she's in an aviary, you must capture her. Place her in a small cage that can be heated by a nearby lamp. The extra warmth may relax her enough to allow her to release the egg. However, if she doesn't expel the egg in two or three hours, you must take more drastic action.

Before capturing her, bring a pot of water to boil on the stove and then turn off the heat. Then pick her up in a dry towel and hold her over the warm (not scalding!) steam. You may also dab a little petroleum jelly on her vent to ease the egg's passage. If the steam and jelly don't work, take her to a vet right away. A beginner should never try to massage an eggbound hen's belly in an attempt to remove the egg.

BREEDING

The Zebra Finch is possibly the easiest of all finches to breed and is often used for fostering.

Since most cases of eggbinding are caused by nutritional deficiencies, you should beef up the diet of all your breeding finches right away. Remember, insufficient calcium, vitamin A, vitamin D, or all three are likely reasons for eggbinding. Check the chapter on diet again for instructions on how to make sure your finches will stay healthier in the future.

To prevent exhausting the finches by asking them to incubate infertile eggs, you can candle the eggs at about seven days after incubation has begun to make sure they're developing properly. A beginner can make a simple candler by enclosing a light bulb within a box with a small hole on top to hold the egg. When you look through the egg at the bright light, you should be able to tell whether it's fertile or not. A fertile egg will contain a dark blob (the developing embryo) and a network of veins that is feeding it. An infertile egg will seem "clear" because nothing is growing inside. Toss it. By the way, it's perfectly normal to find one or two infertile eggs in a clutch.

You can also purchase commercial candlers, either at a local store or through the mail. If you want to candle the eggs of nervous finches, you may want to consider a model currently being offered that's basically a flexible lightstick that allows you to check the eggs without touching them or removing them from the nest.

The eggs will start hatching twelve to sixteen days after incubation begins. Don't be standing there with a stopwatch. The eggs can hatch a little earlier or a little later depending on a number of factors, including how tightly the parents sat on them and what the prevailing temperature is. If it's cool, the eggs will probably hatch a little later than if it's warm.

If everything goes well, 75% to 80% of your fertile eggs should hatch. If your hatchability rate is lower, you need to take another look at your breeding set-up. Did the developing chicks die in the shell because they didn't have enough protein to keep on growing? Next time, make sure your hen has access to plenty of protein food *before* she starts laying. Did the parents toss the eggs or hatchlings out of the nest to die? If they're inexperienced, perhaps you have nothing more to worry about than a case of first-time nerves. Let the finches try again. Chances are, they'll do better. Are you dealing with a pair of rare, touchy finches that won't raise their own young in captivity? Perhaps in the future, you'll have to foster their eggs and chicks under more reliable birds—a technique I'll discuss in a bit more detail in a moment.

As I've already said, interference is a big reason why finches abandon their eggs. Maybe you looked in the nestbox once too often. Or maybe, in an aviary situation, another bird tried to interfere. Watch and see. A curious bully can sabotage nest after nest with its desire to "help." Remove any busybody birds from the aviary, and let them attend to their own breeding efforts in single-pair cages.

What if your finches toss out one of the babies? If it's still alive, warm it in the cup of your hand, perhaps blowing on it a little to speed its recovery. Then put it back in the nest. It's a myth that birds reject babies with the smell of humans on them. Finches can hardly smell at all, so if they reject the baby

Young Gouldian Finches with full crops following a healthy feed.

again, you shouldn't blame yourself for the little one's troubles. After a second rejection, you can guess that the baby was tossed out of the nest intentionally—perhaps because the parents don't think it's healthy or because they don't think they have the right food to raise it properly.

You may be able to save the youngster by placing it in another nest and letting less fussy adults care for it. Or you may have to give it up as lost. If so, try to learn from the experience, but don't be too harsh with yourself. A large proportion of young finches raised in the wild never reach the fledgling stage. That's one of the reasons why finches must attempt to raise so many babies, so that at least a few will survive to replace them.

When a youngster is tossed from the nest or an entire set of eggs is abandoned by fussy exotics, reliable birds like Zebra and Society finches really come into their own. Say one of your costly Lady Goulds casually tosses a valuable chick of unusual color because it "looks funny." ("Funny," to nervous finches, translates as too sickly to waste any effort on.) If you have a pair of Society or Zebra finches with young at about the same age, you can simply add the rejected Lady Gould to that nest and watch the hard-working adoptive parents stuff its crop with goodies.

I should warn you that fostering young finches is fairly controversial. Some breeders feel that you shouldn't try to save the young of fussy parents because these youngsters will perpetuate the fussiness of their parents. Soon, say such breeders, you will establish an entire line of finches that refuse to rear their own young. Fortunately, things aren't usually quite so grim. Youngsters reared under Society or Zebra finches can learn the steadiness of their adoptive parents and become wonderful parents in their turn.

Sometimes, fostered exotic finches will expect their adult mates to look like their adoptive parents. If you let them loose in a mixed aviary, they will choose inappropriate mates. Since you don't want your Lady Goulds trying to breed with your Zebras, you must set up "confused" birds in individual cages with a mate of their own species. In time, given no other choices, the two should settle down together just fine.

Society Finches are devoted parents. Friendly and helpful, they can't help meddling with the chick-rearing of other birds.

BREEDING

No two Society Finches are colored alike.

In order to foster finches successfully, you must give the youngsters to parents who will respond instinctively to the begging motions of the chick. Most popular finches beg by keeping their heads curled low and twisted to one side. Zebras and Society finches will eagerly feed chicks that beg in this fashion, which happily includes many African finches as well as the Australian ones.

However, the Green Singing Finch, Grey Singing Finch, and other members of the Serin (wild canary) family will beg by sticking their necks straight up like canaries. Zebras and Societies don't know how to feed these youngsters. You must foster any rejected Green or Grey Singing Finches to domestic canaries, who should respond to the youngster's canarylike plea for food.

Do not exhaust your reliable parent birds by giving them too many youngsters to care for. Some solicitous Zebras and Societies will literally work themselves to death if you give them the chance. Try to aim for no more than four or five chicks per nest, six in a pinch. Sometimes you may have to discard some of the Society or Zebra eggs in order to make room for more valuable eggs. Don't feel bad about making this choice. Keeping your hard-working parent birds alive and healthy is your top priority. They will get plenty of other chances to raise their own young if you remember that.

Of course, fostering isn't a technique for someone with a single pair of finches in the living room. It requires the time and space to maintain several pairs of foster birds to encourage all of your birds to start breeding at once, so that you will have a working nest or two at the right stage to accept rejects. Control the lighting, food, and supply of nesting material so that all of your finches get the message to start breeding simultaneously.

Can you hand-raise a finch chick that has been rejected by its parents? You can certainly try, but it's hard work and even the experts don't always succeed. To make it work, you'll have to give the tiny youngsters round-the-clock attention for at least two weeks, something that's rarely practical for beginners. If you want to go this route, consult a book or article on handfeeding baby birds for advice.

Hypargos margaritatus, or Rosy Twinspot.

BREEDING

Newborn chicks, two hours old, and eggs about to hatch.

While the parents are feeding babies, you must make sure that they have access to super-nutritious foods at all times. Give the birds all the eggfood, game bird starter or other crumbled protein food, and sprouted seed that they'll take. Of course, finches that feed their youngsters on live insects should have plenty of those available. Small grubs and "mini" mealworms are great for finches. However, too many mealworms can upset the calcium balance in a bird's body. If you notice your birds feeding mealworms to the exclusion of all else, call your vet and ask for a prescription for a calcium powder that you can sprinkle on the worms before feeding. If that isn't practical—perhaps there isn't an avian vet in your area—you can make your own high calcium powder from eggshells. Sterilize the shells in the oven and powder them in the blender.

If you are interested in breeding rare finches, in showing your finches, or in developing new types of finches, you will probably want to band your birds. A permanent closed band that remains on the finch for life is the best way you can prove that you bred the finch yourself. By referring to the numbers on the band, you can also keep accurate records on the finch's bloodline, health, and characteristics.

43

You must decide ahead of time if you plan to close-band your birds. Not only must you order the bands in advance, you must establish a routine of checking the nest each day so that the parent birds will be accustomed to your interference. Otherwise, they may be so distressed by a big hand creeping into the nest to grab babies for banding that they toss out the newly banded chicks.

Place the bands on the young birds when they're between four and seven days old, slipping it carefully over their toes. Things will go a bit more smoothly if you pass the band over the front three toes first, then over the foot pad, and then over the rear toe while it's being held gently against the leg. Within a few days, the toes will grow too large to allow the band to come off.

If you have no reason to band your finches, then don't feel you must. With any band, there's always a chance that it can catch on something and injure the bird. It's a small risk, but one you shouldn't take if you don't have to.

Incidentally, if you don't band your finches when they are small, you can band them later with so-called "open" bands. Since these nonpermanent bands have seams, they aren't proof that you bred the bird. However, they make it easy to identify birds "at a glance" since you can mark all birds of a certain bloodline or sex with the same bright, easy-to-see color.

In about three weeks, the young finches may leave the nest. However, they are certainly not ready to care for themselves, so don't separate them from their parents yet. Weaning is a gradual process that may take another month. While the babies are learning to crack seeds and pick up food, their parents should continue to feed and care for them.

Occasionally, the parents will become impatient with the juveniles because they want to start work on a new nest. If the hen is plucking the youngsters' feathers or otherwise harassing them, remove the babies and the cock to another cage. He can "finish off" the juveniles on his own, something he would often do in the wild anyway, while the hen gets on with the next nest.

Once the finches have raised two or three clutches in a row, it's wise to discourage them from breeding for a while.

A pair of White Zebra Finches. These are bred in captivity and are not albinos, as shown by the dark eye. The female is heavier.

Gradually decrease the amount of light and protein food, and remove the nesting materials. Your hard-working birds deserve a rest so that they can build up their bodies and nutrient reserves for another successful season.

There are hundreds of species of the small, active seed-eaters known as finches. However, beginners usually start with one of the most popular breeds. You're likely to find useful information about your first finches somewhere in the following list.

SPECIES

THE BIG TWO

I've already said a fair amount about Zebra and Society finches. These adaptable little birds reproduce eagerly and efficiently, making great parents to their own chicks and those of other finches. Even if the diet and care aren't perfect, these finches can thrive and raise young. And they do offer many colorful and crested varieties that keep the hobby interesting even for a veteran breeder. For all these reasons, Zebra or Society finches are the best choice for a beginner.

The Society finch (*Lonchura domestica*) is a completely domesticated bird that was developed in Asia over three hundred years ago. There is no such bird in the wild. We have lost the secret of how the original breeders developed Societies, but it's believed that they must have crossed several closely related species of finches in order to create the new bird. Societies thrive in captivity on simple diets because that's what they were bred to do. "Society" is a particularly apt name for them, since they are friendly birds who love to get involved in everybody's business. However, they are also sometimes called Bengalese finches.

Since Societies can't be sexed by eye, you must place them in a large flight and let them pick out their own partners. Make sure the flight is large enough to support the breeding efforts of four or more pairs. If you put just two or three pairs together, it's too easy for them to develop an organized "peck-

Facing page:
The Gouldian Finch is even lovelier in person than this excellent photograph can convey . . . and delightful to own.

ing order" that results in the "bottom" bird being harrassed to death. Fortunately, finches can't seem to count above six!

The wild Zebra finch (*Taeniopygia guttata*) lives in the arid grasslands of Australia. The "normal" Zebra finch found in every pet shop looks like the wild bird. However, it has also been bred in captivity long enough to make it a reliable breeder and cheerful pet. Because its home environment was relatively rugged, Zebras also do well on simpler diets than most other finches. Easily sexed, Zebras can be bred in cages or in aviaries. Again, if you go the aviary route, have more than three pairs in the flight.

Because they are such self-confident busybodies, Zebras and Societies can prove annoying to more delicate finches. In most cases, you shouldn't ask your exotic finches to share quarters with these species.

THE CANARY AND ITS RELATIVES

The domestic Canary (*Serinus canarius domesticus*) is an extremely popular and hardy bird kept primarily for its song and cheerful colors. There are many types of Canaries which are constantly being improved by breeders who exhibit their birds on the show circuit. Should you visit a bird show—something I highly recommend to familiarize yourself with the look and sound of top-quality birds—you will be overwhelmed by

The exceptional Blue Lizard Canary.

An amazing Parisian Frilled Canary. One can be sure a bird such as this was never found in the wild.

the varieties of Canaries present. Red Canaries, yellow Canaries, crested Canaries, lizard Canaries, frilled Canaries . . . I could go on and on. Suffice it to say that Canaries can be a hobby all their own. The basic finch care described in this book is fine if you're just keeping a pair or two. But if you get bitten by the Canary bug, you will want to acquire some of the voluminous literature available on this interesting little bird.

Canaries are alert and interested in people, but I still suggest that you buy a friend for your male singing Canary. All finches, Societies included, are happier if they can play with someone their own size.

The Wild Canary (*Serinus canarius canarius*) isn't very popular in aviculture because it's quite plain next to the domesticated Canary. However, the Green Singing Finch (*Serinus mozambicus*) is a close relative of the Canary that's quite popular among finch fans. You will find it easier to cage-breed Green Singers that come from captive-bred stock. Wild birds imported from Africa can be hesitant to breed in captivity unless you provide them with a planted aviary.

It's easy to sex adult Green Singers since the female wears a "necklace" of dark spots on her throat. However, young juveniles of both sexes also possess spots. You will have to wait until a youngster is some three to four months old before you'll know what sex it is. At that age, bright yellow will begin breaking through the spots on the throats of the males.

A small quantity of live insects, such as a couple of small mealworms a day, will encourage the Green Singers to breed. You can also teach younger birds (and some older ones) to sing more like Canaries if you play them a Canary song album or tape on a regular basis.

Canaries are popular songbirds, easy to keep, and available in a kaleidoscope of colors.

The Purple Grenadier is a rare and expensive when available native of East Africa. Male and female birds are shown.

OTHER POPULAR AFRICAN FINCHES

Unlike the serins, the following African finches can be fostered under Zebra or Society finches instead of under Canaries. These species are admired mainly for their attractive colors and pert personalities rather than for their songs. Since many finches are still imported from Africa, you may have a wild-caught pair that needs a little more understanding than a captive-bred pair that's used to people and the common pet foods. Some wild-caught African finches may not realize that eggfood is just as protein-rich as insects and will therefore refuse to try to rear their young on it. Because the captive-bred finches are sturdier and easier to breed, expect to pay more for them.

One popular group of African finches is the waxbills, a colorful tribe of weaver-finches from around the equator. Because of their lovely blue color, Cordon Bleus (*Uraeginthus bengalus*) are probably the most popular of the African waxbills.

They're easy to sex once they're mature, since the male has a distinctive bright red cheek patch to distinguish him from the female. Wild-caught Cordon Bleus are most likely to breed in an aviary well planted with seeding grasses and supplied with live insects. Steadier pairs, especially if they're captive-bred themselves, may reproduce in a cage provided with a covered nest. You should always be sure to give them dry grass for nesting and lots of egg or other high-protein food. They can't "get by" on a seed-only diet for very long.

The Violet-eared Waxbill (*Uraeginthus grantinus*) and the Purple Grenadier (*Uraeginthus iathinogaster*) are two close relatives of the Cordon Bleu that require similar care. The Violet-eared is named for its large violet ear patch. The adult males have a distinctive black throat patch the females lack. The male Purple Grenadier has a brilliant purple breast, while the female sports more subtle shades of light blue and brown.

The Green Singing Finch, a charming bird, is well-known for its beautiful song and attractive coloration.

Both species usually won't breed if they don't have a good supply of their favorite wild insects. Terry Dunham, an expert on finch breeding, convinced Violet-ears to breed by offering live termites—a technique that might be too hard on your nerves unless the aviary is detached from your home!

If you can get your Cordon Bleus, Violet-ears, or Purple Grenadiers to lay fertile eggs, you may increase your chances of success by fostering the clutch to Zebra finches. Societies often seem to think that the dark young of Cordon Bleus and Purple Grenadiers, in particular, don't look healthy enough to bother with.

The White-Hooded Nun, another attentive parent, can be successfully used for fostering.

The Gold-Breasted Waxbill (*Amandava subflava*), the smallest waxbill, is a tiny, delicate jewel of a bird. The adult male's breast is a darker shade of gold to orange-red than is the female's. Tiny and active, these waxbills require the best quality foods. In addition to their seeds, they should have an egg mash or other high protein food available at all times. Tiny live insects make a valuable treat.

Because they are so small, many finch cages won't hold Gold-Breasts. You may have to make your own cage of half-inch or quarter-inch hardware cloth in order to make sure these tiny jewels don't slip away from you.

The Strawberry Finch (*Amandava amandava*) comes from both Asia and Africa. Unlike most non-serins, the male

Strawberry Finch is a sweet singer rather than a quiet chirper. These finches are also unusual in that the male loses its strawberry-colored plumage when it's out of breeding season. At this time, the male and female look much alike. A male can lose his lovely coloring permanently if kept indoors under artificial lights and fed substandard food, so keep the diet excellent whenever he starts to molt.

The Orange-Cheeked Waxbill (*Estrilda melpoda*) is a popular waxbill that's rather hard to sex. Both males and females possess the bright orange cheeks. However, if you can be sure that you're comparing two birds of the same age, the one with the slightly larger cheek patch is probably the male.

The Cutthroat Finch (*Amadina fasciata*) is a striking finch that's inexpensive and readily available. Only males have the distinctive ribbon of red on the throat that gives this species its name.

Silverbills (*Euodice malabarica*) are finches of subtle coloring. Since the sexes look alike, you will probably have to colony breed these birds in an aviary. Fortunately, Silverbills are tolerant, peaceful birds that do well with other kinds of finches. The biggest problem may be that a busybody Society Finch decides to take over the nest, responsibilities and all!

There are two subspecies of Silverbills that are commonly offered for sale to beginners, Indian Silverbills (*E. m. malabarira*) and African Silverbills (*E. m. cantans*). They aren't easy for a beginner to tell apart, and since they can interbreed to produce fertile young, you may never realize that you've paired an African to an Indian. Look for a black rump; if it's there, you have an African. If you can, try not to interbreed the two subspecies. In a world where species and subspecies are lost every year to extinction, aviculturists have a special responsibility to make sure that natural forms are well established in captivity before they try to hybridize them.

Again, all of these attractive waxbills will require long, dry grass for nesting material and a high-protein diet if you want them to breed.

Gouldian Finches need more protein than some of the other finches for good health and egg-laying.

LADY GOULDIAN FINCHES

Many bird lovers will tell you point blank that Lady Goulds (*Chloebia gouldiae*) are the world's most beautiful finches. Naturally decked out in the Mardi Gras colors, the normal males sport purple breasts, yellow bellies, and green backs. The females wear a more subdued shade of the same outfit. In the wild, most Gouldians have black heads but the red-headed variety does crop up fairly often.

In recent years, breeders have developed a rainbow of Lady Gould mutations. Although this species' natural beauty would seem hard to improve on, the new varieties certainly possess their own quiet appeal. The white-breasted Gouldian, for example, may appeal to those who find the natural purple breast a bit garish. Other varieties you may see include yellow-headed, rose breasted, blue breasted, blue bodied, and white bodied. And hard-working breeders are expanding the list all the time.

Lady Goulds are quite expensive for two reasons—the high demand and the fact that they are captive-bred. If you want to breed these finches, you would be very wise to get some experience with one of the less costly finches first. Zebras are a good choice if you plan to go on to Lady Goulds because they come from a similar environment and share many of the same quirks.

55

Although Lady Goulds do have a "prima donna" reputation, they're not really difficult birds. Years ago, when people tried to maintain them on low-protein diets, they lost a large proportion of their Gouldians during the molt. No finch can replace its old feathers without an adequate supply of protein—and "adequate," Lady Goulds, is quite a bit more than most people were used to feeding their Zebras. By now, though, you should know enough about nutrition to keep your Goulds in the pink.

Gouldians aren't very hard to breed if you have some experience with other finches. You can breed them in colonies in a large aviary or set up pairs in individual cages with four cubic feet of volume or more. They usually get along well with Society and Zebra finches if you must mix these birds in the same flight. You would have to provide the whole aviary with more protein food than you might if it contained just the Zebras, but that's really no big deal. Besides, it's always wise to accustom your Societies and Zebras to a protein-rich diet so that they will feed any fostered young properly.

Lady Goulds may lay in open or covered nests, but they tend to favor the covered kind. Since they usually copulate within the nestbox, give them something a little bigger than you'd offer a Zebra or Society. Otherwise, the male may not have enough room to mount the female, leading to clutch after clutch of infertile eggs.

Some breeders end up hatching out many more males than females. Robert G. Black, the finch expert, reports that after he installed full spectrum lighting in his Gouldian area, he went from producing mostly males to producing a bit more than half females. If, as he speculates, the presence of invisible wavelengths of light are responsible for the change, keeping your Lady Goulds in an outdoor aviary should have a similar effect.

OTHER AUSTRALIAN FINCHES

Except for the ubiquitous Zebra, most Australian finches are more expensive than the African finches. Since Australia stopped exporting its wildlife in the early 1960's, all Australian finches sold in other countries today must come from

The Longtailed Grassfinch, from Australia is among the best of all aviary subjects.

captive-bred stock. That's actually good news, though. As we've seen, captive-bred finches are easier for beginners (and everyone else!) to breed—and the higher prices mean you're rewarded for your efforts when you succeed.

Even if you're just interested in keeping a pair as pets, the captive-bred Australians have some advantages. Since they're used to people, they are steadier and happier in cages or smaller flights. And, since their parents usually had to bring them up on eggfood, they don't look for live insect treats during the molt or other stressful periods.

The Shafttail or Longtailed Grassfinch (*Poephila acuticauda*) is a sleek Australian named for its tapering tail that ends in two bare central shafts. It isn't easy to sex these birds, but the male generally has a broader black throat patch than the female. They get along well with other birds and can be bred in both cage and aviary. If they lay more than five fertile eggs in a clutch, foster the extras to Societies to prevent neglect of the young or exhaustion of the parents.

The Parson Finch (*Poephila cincta*) and the Masked Grass Finch (*Poephila personata*) are close relatives of the Shafttail. The Masked Grass Finch looks like a Shafttail without the elongated bare shafts growing out of its tail, while the Parson Finch can be distinguished by its square, short tail. Don't keep

these three very similar species in the same aviary, or they may try to interbreed, leaving you with a mongrel.

Like the Shafttail, female Parsons have smaller bibs than their mates. Both sexes of the Masked Grass Finch look alike, although the male may sing a little. Fortunately, they can be colony bred in a large aviary and allowed to choose their own partners. The care of Parsons and Masked Grass Finches is similar to that of the Shafttails, although the Masked Grass Finch can be more difficult to breed.

Star Finches (*Bathilda ruficauda* or *Poephila ruficauda*) are interesting little birds marked with spots or "stars" on their breasts, throats, and cheeks. Although a yellow-faced mutation is available, beginners are more likely to encounter Stars whose faces are drab due to being kept indoors. To prevent the bright red face from fading, supply a full-spectrum light source or keep the Stars outdoors. If the female lays more than four fertile eggs, it's best to foster the extras to Societies.

I think the Owl or Bicheno's Finch (*Poephila bichenovi*) is as attractive in its own right as the Lady Gould. Its crisp patterns and simple colors are a far cry from the "Easter egg" plumage of the Lady Gould, but its owlish face and neat chest bars give it plenty of attention-getting power. Owls are hard to sex. If you have a number of them to look at, you can see that some birds have wider, more striking bands than others. These birds will be the males.

Owl Finches prefer open nests to enclosed boxes in most cases. The parents tend to be very devoted to the rearing of young.

In the wild, European Bullfinches pair for life.

Owls are usually peaceful in a mixed aviary but sometimes they'll quarrel with others of their own kind. To avoid problems, keep only one pair in each flight unless it's really huge.

Diamond Sparrows (*Stagonopleura guttata*) are large finches, not sparrows. These calm, cheerful birds often live near humans in their Australian homeland. In captivity, they get along well with other finches in a mixed aviary. They can get obese if kept in cages, so don't overfeed them on oily seed or mealworms.

TWO POPULAR EUROPEAN FINCES

The European Bullfinch (*Pyrrhula pyrrhula*) is a gorgeous bird with a black cap and face mask and a lovely pink breast. The female looks much the same except that her underparts are more soft gray than pink. Although both sexes look thicker and sturdier than most other finches, their hardy appearance is a bit deceptive. They will sicken and die on a seed-only or a seed-and-greens-only diet. To keep them fit, you need to offer an assortment of live insects and small berries in addition to the standard finch diet. Waxworms and other small grubs may not keep around the house for weeks the way that mealworms do, but they remain an important treat for your bullfinches. Before you offer wild berries to your birds, make sure that they're nonpoisonous. Rowan berries are favorite

treats, and you can easily find small blackberries growing in many areas of the United States. You are most likely to breed your bullfinches if you keep a single pair in a well-planted aviary.

Is the extra work worth it? People who have taught their agreeable Bullfinches to whistle popular tunes such as "Silent Night" certainly think so.

The European Goldfinch (*Carduelis carduelis*) is a pretty songbird with a red face and a slim, pretty body. These calm, curious finches make good pets who will sing happily from a cage. However, they will breed much more readily in a planted aviary. To check the sex of a Goldfinch, look at the wing feathers between the shoulders and the bend of the wing. The adult males should have some black in this area, while adult females and juveniles will show more of a grayish-brown.

A WORLD OF POSSIBILITIES

We've just begun to touch on a few of the more popular finches. Yet, you can already see that the finch hobby is one that can grow as large or stay as small as you care to make it. Perhaps a quick look at a few unusual species will give you an idea of what finch fanatics may be letting themselves in for!

Consider the beautiful and rare Parrot Finches. Named

The gorgeous Australian Painted Finch.

SPECIES

Regardless of what kind of finch you choose, you will have many, many hours of pleasure and companionship from these wonderful little birds.

for their gaudy feathers, these Pacifican birds are costly legends. The breeders who figure out how to reliably reproduce these coveted little finches will certainly be amply rewarded.

Another interesting bird is the Quail Finch (*Ortygospiza atricollis*), a bizarre finch that acts like a quail and even looks a little like one. Like quail, they prefer to stay on the ground and therefore need a dirt or turf aviary floor in order to keep their feet healthy. They dirtbathe in a pie plate of sand rather than splashing in a tub bath the way other finches do.

Perhaps the most challenging group of finches is the whydahs. These interesting little birds have some curious reproductive habits. During the breeding season, the males develop showy plumage and long graceful tails to attract the attention of the females, who remain the same sparrowlike color all year round. However, the females aren't hard-working "drabs" who do all the work and miss all the fun. Instead, they cleverly lay their eggs in the nests of some other finches and let someone else bring up baby—a natural sort of fostering referred to as nest parasitism.

61

The unusual and beautiful Quail Finch.

Because they prefer to parasitize specific species, you can't just hope that your whydahs will lay their eggs in the nest of your Zebra finches. I'm afraid it's a bit trickier than that. For instance, the Pintailed Whydah (*Vidua macroura*) prefers to leave its eggs in the care of St. Helena Waxbills, a rarely bred species in itself. Other whydahs parasitize Melba finches, Violet-eared Waxbills, and Purple Grenadiers. So a recipe for breeding whydahs would have to begin: "First you become an African finch expert . . ."

Of course, you don't have to go that far to enjoy your finches. You may be perfectly content with a single cage of companionable singers or pert show-offs. With finches, you really do have a whole world of choices.

The following books by T.F.H. Publications are available at pet shops everywhere.

FINCHES AND SOFT-BILLED BIRDS By Henry Bates and Robert Busenbark (H-908)

The classic reference on finches and soft-bills. Every important cage bird (except parrots) is discussed and illustrated in color. No other

SUGGESTED READING

book in any language has so many birds known in the pet world. Used extensively all over the world as an identification guide, this book also covers all the fundamentals of maintaining and breeding these species.

Illustrated with 246 color and 159 black-and-white photos. Hard cover, 5½ x 8", 735 pp.

THE COMPLETE CAGE AND AVIARY BIRD HANDBOOK By David Alderton (H-1087)

Each section contains remarks about feeding, general care, and breeding, followed by species commentaries. Opening with a chapter on avian biology, subsequent chapters cover birds as pets and generally discuss housing, feeding, management, illness, breeding, and the genetics of the color mutations. Drawings and photos help the reader to visualize anatomical structures, the design of aviaries and furnishings, and the paradigms of inheritance.

Illustrated with 167 color and 20 black-and-white photos and more than 60 drawings. Hard cover, 7½ x 9½", 160 pp.

Index

Page numbers in bold type represent the location of photographs.